Britain's Demographic Challenge

Britain's Demographic Challenge

The implications of the UK's rapidly
increasing population

Lord Hodgson of Astley Abbotts

CIVITAS

First Published September 2017

© Civitas 2017
55 Tufton Street
London SW1P 3QL

email: books@civitas.org.uk

ISBN 978-1-906837-91-4

Independence: Civitas: Institute for the Study of Civil Society is a registered educational charity (No. 1085494) and a company limited by guarantee (No. 04023541). Civitas is financed from a variety of private sources to avoid over-reliance on any single or small group of donors.

All publications are independently refereed. All the Institute's publications seek to further its objective of promoting the advancement of learning. The views expressed are those of the authors, not of the Institute.

Typeset by
Typetechnique

Printed in Great Britain by
4edge Limited, Essex

Contents

Foreword

This pamphlet would not have been possible without the help of various contributors. Chief among them have been Alex House and Hugh Ellis from the Town and Country Planning Association, Michael O'Connor as well as various officials in the Office of National Statistics and in several local councils. As one might expect a pamphlet on this topic has given rise to a tidal wave of figures and data. To organise this tsunami and to sift through the noise, I have to thank Adam Beazley, a recent graduate from Hull University, who whilst on a year's secondment to the House of Lords assisted with research and so helped get this pamphlet over the finishing line. Many other friends and colleagues have contributed – often without knowing – as I have taken the opportunity to test my thoughts and ideas on them. The conclusions are, of course, mine alone.

Over an extended period of time I gathered information on the UK's demographics. I have supplemented this by attending lectures and demography related events. Additionally, I canvassed a number of experts on the subject. In writing this pamphlet the objective was first to collate and interpret the information gathered. Much of the data used is drawn from the Office of National Statistics and other official sources; however, there are some instances of author calculations. The evidence was then used to structure and frame the arguments which have then been buttressed by numerous books, reports and articles.

Completing this pamphlet has been taxing and thought-provoking; taxing because the range of data available is almost infinite and thought-provoking because it raises issues that will shape our country for many years into the future. It is therefore a subject which deserves serious debate, not just in government, but amongst the wider general public. If this pamphlet helps encourage such a discussion I shall regard it as having achieved its objectives.

Lord Hodgson of Astley Abbotts
July 2017

Author

Robin Granville Hodgson (The Lord Hodgson of Astley Abbotts CBE) grew up in the little Shropshire village of Astley Abbotts. After graduating from St Peter's College, Oxford, he spent five years in North America where he took an MBA at the Wharton School of Finance.

On his return to the UK he set up Granville and Co, a specialist private equity and investment banking business focussed on the mid-market sector. After 30 years as Chief Executive and then Chairman, the business was sold to a US investment bank. Since then he has invested in and chaired a numbered of early stage companies.

In 1972, he was adopted as the Conservative parliamentary candidate for Walsall North. He fought the two 1974 General Elections and in 1976 he was elected MP for the seat at a by-election following the disappearance of the sitting member John Stonehouse.

After losing the seat in 1979 he became an active volunteer member of the Conservative Party ending up as Deputy Chairman of the party in the 1990s.

He was created a life peer in 2000. His particular focus, in addition to trade, industry and finance, has been the charity and voluntary sector. He has authored a number of reports for the Government on the sector – most recently on the regulation of third party campaigning. He is an officer of several all-party parliamentary groups and is currently chairing a cross party House of Lords committee looking into citizenship and civic engagement.

He is married to Fiona, who as Baroness Hodgson of Abinger is a peer in her own right, and they have four children.

Overview

- In the year ending 30 June 2016 the population of the United Kingdom increased by 538,500, equivalent to 1,475 people per day. At the current rate of housing occupation (2.3 people per dwelling), this will require the construction of 641 dwellings per day – 27 per hour or one every two minutes, night and day.

- The Office of National Statistics' principal projection is that the population of the UK will increase by 9.7 million to reach 74.3 million by 2039. On the above metric that will require 4.25 million more dwellings or one every three minutes during that time period.

- Demography has a 'long fuse' – policy changes take at least 10 years to have any significant impact. So, the result of any changes made now will not be seen much before 2030.

- The challenges of population growth result from changes in absolute numbers; not from changes in racial, religious or cultural background. So, this pamphlet considers the impact of the absolute numbers of population growth on the economic, social and environmental development of the UK, not of changes to the racial, religious or cultural background of its inhabitants.

- The potential increase in the population poses particular challenges for the UK given its geographical constraints.

- The emergence of English as the lingua franca of the world – especially the world of technology – has increased the UK's gravitational pull.

- The average daily increase of 1,475 people breaks down into 529 from a natural increase (excess of births over deaths), 518 net arrivals from the EU, 537 net arrivals from elsewhere in the world balanced by 137 net departing UK citizens.

- The data on which much of the demographic debate is imprecise. The e-Borders system is still not fully operational; many of the surveys themselves are quite small and completed voluntarily. And some data reaches dramatically different conclusions. For example, in 2016 824,000 new National Insurance numbers were issued to individuals from overseas – this is 21% higher than the reported level of gross immigration of 630,000.

- The rate of growth in the UK's population has increased by the higher fertility rate of new arrivals. One quarter of the births in the UK in 2011 were to women born outside the UK.

- England, which averages 420 people per sq. km, is far more densely populated than Scotland (69), Northern Ireland (136) and Wales (149). These figures are not adjusted for essentially uninhabitable areas of mountains etc.

- Over the period 1990-2015, England's population has grown faster (13.9% increase) than Scotland (6.2%) and Wales (8.0%). England's growth has been focused on the southern half of the country, London (27.6%), East (19.5%) and the South West (17.3%).

- The UK (269 people per sq. km) is more densely populated than France (105) and Germany (229); England alone has 420 people per sq. km.

- Based on the ONS principal projection of the UK's population in 2039 (9.7 million increase), the UK population density will increase by 14% from 269 to 305 people per sq. km. England alone is estimated to increase from 420 to 486.

- If this increase comes about it will emphasise the difference in population densities compared with France and Germany. By 2080 the UK will have become the most populous country in Europe and be 1.5 times more densely populated than Germany and 2.7 times than France.

- 9.7 million people is a figure difficult to imagine. To put this in context, this is equivalent to 3.5 times the population of Greater Manchester or 1.7 times that of the West Midlands conurbation.

- The challenge is not just about the spatial requirements of housing. There will also need to be new hospitals, schools, employment opportunities, leisure facilities, roads and general infrastructure.

- The impact of these changes will be felt primarily at local community level – though these may vary widely in different parts of the country.

- The economic case for population increase is based on total GDP. The right measure should surely be GDP per head. Mass lower skill immigration does not increase GDP per head and indeed can lead to the 'crowding out' of our settled population.

- Another challenge is the change to the dependency ratio – those of working age compared to those either too young or too old to work. However, improvements in technology and raising the retirement ages may well offset some of these impacts.

- Too often the issues of population growth are looked at only through an economic prism. There are quality of life arguments as well.

- There is a social contract that bonds us all together in society which is underpinned by a sense of 'fairness'. Too rapid an increase in population may challenge the concept of what is 'fair'.

The Way Forward

- Create a strategic policy framework under a Minister for Demography to work cross-departmentally so as to guide and inform policy matters generally.

- Involve local government in all aspects of policy development.

- Inform and encourage a wide debate amongst the general public.

- Establish a proper evidence base on all aspects of population growth.

- Learn from other nations that have seen rapid population changes – both increases or decreases.

Introduction

The past twelve months have seen significant shifts in the tectonic plates of British society. The referendum campaign, a fiercely fought General Election (which produced an unexpected result) and the carrying out of four terrorist attacks (allegedly mostly implemented by individuals born in this country) have brought to the front of the public mind a series of challenging policy issues including the maintenance of social cohesion, the impact of relative poverty, progress on increasing levels of integration and aspiration and the need to control our borders.

But no-one has attempted to set these challenges into the context of the rapidly growing *absolute* number of people in this country. It is hard to believe that this has not impacted on the above issues, or that it will not in the future.

This pamphlet attempts to explain the challenges and opportunities of likely future overall population growth for the United Kingdom. It will be particularly important that these implications are borne in mind as the UK's negotiating team begins to frame the new relationship between the EU and this country.

Setting the Scene

In the year ending 30 June 2016 the population of the United Kingdom is estimated to have increased by an average of 1,475 per day – a total increase in the year of 538,500.[1] It means that a small town or large village, with a population of roughly 10,355, is being put on to the map of the UK every week.

This rate of increase must be expected to have implications for the country as a whole and, no less importantly, for its 'settled population'. For example, currently in this country, according to the 2011 census, there are 2.3 people per dwelling.[2] We surely should not expect to treat our future residents any less well. So, to house 1,475 people we need 641 new dwellings per day – that means 27 per hour or nearly one every two minutes night and day. This is without allowing for any improvements to our existing housing stock.

The increase in our population comes from two main sources. First the 'natural increase' (the excess of births over deaths) which accounted for 529 of the 1,475 (35.9%) and, second, the excess of immigration over emigration, which accounted for 920 of the 1,475 (62.4%). So, in considering the challenge of the future absolute levels of population, control of immigration will not provide all the answers. Nevertheless, past migration patterns affect the natural increase – higher immigration increases the growth rate given that migrants are predominately younger. Thus, an Office of National Statistics (ONS) report from 2014 used the latest census data for England and Wales to show births to women themselves born outside the UK accounted for 25.5% of all births in 2011 up from 16.4% in the previous census (2001).[3]

The population increase in 2016 was not extraordinary – it continued the trend of recent years. Though it should be borne in mind that the trend of recent years (certainly the past one or two decades) has been extraordinary migration-wise compared with any previous time in recorded history. So, what of the next quarter-century?

The science of demographic projections – in particular over the medium and longer term – is hedged about with uncertainties. But the current ONS mid estimate suggests that over the full 25-year period of it latest projection, the UK population will increase by 15.0% (9.7m) to reach 74.3m by mid-2039, with an annual average growth rate of 0.6%.[4] On the housing metric given above of 2.3 people per dwelling, this means that we will need 4.25m more dwellings by 2039, or one every three minutes for the next 25 years.

Some argue that the challenge as regards housing could be largely solved by addressing the current 'under occupation' of housing. This spare capacity is alleged to result from baby boomers continuing to occupy the houses in which they brought up children who have long left home, a trend which is accentuated by the number of them whose partners have died but who nevertheless remain in their family homes alone. The problem can be simply stated but solving it requires a degree of state direction which would surely be unacceptable to the British people. The level of opposition to the 'spare bedroom tax' – a policy designed only to redress public subsidy of overlarge dwellings – gives a foretaste of what the reaction might be.

A particular challenge of demography is the length of time it takes for any policy change to have an impact. For example, if immigration were, at a stroke, to be reduced dramatically it would be some years before the full consequent reduction in population worked its way through the system. The same delayed effect applies as regards any government policies which might, directly or indirectly, result in smaller families. So, a nudge on the demographic tiller takes at least ten and probably twenty-five years before the full impact can be judged.

So, what will happen demographically to this country up to about 2025 is largely set in stone. Beyond that date, the position is less certain. This 'long fuse', as well as the highly emotive nature of the topic, explains why politicians of all parties have been reluctant to be drawn into any debate about the likely consequences of the projected increases in the population over the next 25 years, particularly the interaction between economic and non-economic factors and especially as regards any possible impact on social cohesion.

But no matter how sensitive a topic this may be, one cannot ignore an underlying public concern about the issue. If this is not addressed calmly and dispassionately wilder views and opinions may gain ground.

This pamphlet is written by a layman for laymen and as such runs the risk of over-simplification. It begins by attempting to clarify the terms of the debate. It goes on to identify some of the likely implications for the United Kingdom as a whole, as well as for Scotland, Wales and Northern Ireland together with the regions of England and draws some comparison of the anticipated projected levels of future populations of other EU countries. It looks in more detail at what the future may hold for four very different communities in England and Scotland if the ONS projections prove accurate. It examines some of the most frequently raised arguments for and against increasing our population. It concludes by listing some possible policy options – which might help prepare the country for what lies ahead.

It is *definitely not* a pamphlet focusing on immigration though immigration plays a part. It is *definitely not* a pamphlet about the racial make-up of the country – it is about absolute numbers – and where the pamphlet refers to 'settled population' it means precisely that, irrespective of race, colour, creed etc.

It has nevertheless to be admitted that the term 'settled population' does not have a neat definition. 'Settling' is not about physical presence alone, it contains elements of expectation and attitude. Some individuals may have lived in the UK for, say, ten years but have no intention of 'settling' here permanently. Others have been here one year and never intend to move again. Still others find their intentions change as they age or their children move overseas.

At root the purpose of the pamphlet is to encourage public debate. This is an important issue which will one way or another affect fundamentally the lives of future generations. Should what lies ahead cause public concern? To answer that question, we need to consider the evidence. What would surely be unacceptable would be for people to find themselves in a situation the implications of which for reasons of reticence or sensitivity had not been the subject of an honest and open analysis.

1

Clarifying the terms of debate

This chapter examines certain key aspects of the demographic debate as well as the terminology used.

1.1 Historic attitudes to population levels

For many years it has been a popular view among policymakers that a growing population brings many advantages. It is argued that larger populations should result in a larger economy with the attendant increase in economic power and influence. At a more basic level a larger population was seen as being able to provide larger armed forces which, in the ultimate, could enforce the country's will in the wider world or could better protect it from threats by others. Finally, a growing population was seen as evidence of an underlying dynamic in the nation both because of its implicit virility and because the arrival of new people from overseas was evidence of a country that attracted people from elsewhere.

But the constraints of space and resources together with the emergence of new ways for a nation to build its influence – the phenomenon of 'soft power' – are now making themselves felt. In consequence 'the bigger the better' argument is increasingly being questioned in terms both of effectiveness and sustainability.

1.2 Particular challenges for the United Kingdom

The United Kingdom has been and remains an attractive place for people to live and work. The emergence of English as the lingua franca of the world – especially the world of technology – has given the UK a natural gravitational pull. Further, the administrative and financial structures linked to a natural entrepreneurial flair amongst the population have made the UK an attractive place to do business.

No less important is what can be described as the 'ethos' of the country. I use this as a collective noun to describe the values a country holds most dear. Voltaire wrote, 'Every people has its character, as well as every man',[1] but sadly he did not provide a collective term! Each one of us will have our own individual list of those values that made us either stay here or come here from abroad; most will include freedom of speech, freedom of worship, an independent judiciary, an administration that is to all intents and purposes free of corruption, a respect for the rule of law, tolerance, a sense of humour and, last but not least, a high regard for fairness.

But these very attractions lead to challenges. The UK is small geographically, particularly when one discounts its essentially uninhabitable areas of mountains, moorland etc. So, density of population is becoming a real issue – such a constraint does not exist in the United States or indeed many other European countries which can, in consequence, take a much more relaxed view of population growth.

These challenges are accentuated by the bias within the UK towards London and the South East – despite great efforts by successive governments, the pull of London appears, if anything, to have increased in recent years.

1.3 Categories of population change

It is important to drill down into the two constituent parts of population change. This requires us to wrestle with data sources that are not always as precise as one might wish. First, there is the *natural increase* – the excess of births over deaths. That at least is a simple, unchallengeable number. Its future trend will be determined on the one hand by the extent to which life expectancy changes – increasing or reducing the number of deaths – the other by changes in the total fertility rate (TFR) – increasing or reducing the average number of children born to each woman.

Secondly there is *net migration*. This is made up of two components – immigration and emigration. The immigration figures require closer analysis. There are arrivals from the EU – now accounting for slightly more than half the gross immigration figure – membership of which, of course, requires free movement of labour. But the overall EU figure itself needs to be broken down between the other earlier-joining western European member states and the later arrivals from eastern Europe – consisting of Poland, Latvia, Lithuania, Czech Republic, Slovakia, Slovenia, Estonia, Hungary, Bulgaria and Romania.

Then there are arrivals from the rest of the world – a hugely diverse group of countries with very different historic ties and connections with the UK. As of 2013, the non-EU countries with the largest UK populations were, in order: India, Pakistan, South Africa, Nigeria, Bangladesh and the USA.[2]

There are *students* – argued to be an important component in Britain's soft power armoury. Under the UN categorisation, adopted by the UK, students are defined as migrants.[3]

There are *returning emigrants* – people whose work overseas has come to an end or for a variety of other reasons have decided to return home to the UK.

Finally, on the other balance in the scale there are *emigrants*. These will include individuals who have been working in the UK and wish to return to their home country; members of the settled population who have taken work overseas on a temporary or a permanent basis; and finally, people, usually older, who have decided to join relatives overseas or retired to live in sunnier climes.

So, the 1,475 per day increase in population in 2016 breaks down as in Table 1.1 (the full details are shown in Appendix I Table AI.1).

In summary, Table 1.1 shows that the *net* increase in the UK's population on a daily basis is made up of 529 more births than deaths, 518 more people from the EU and 537 more people from outside the EU entering than leaving balanced by 137 more British leaving than entering. It needs to be understood that this latter category is likely to be a wide-ranging group – some seeking the better climate of, say, Australia or others returning to family roots in, say, Jamaica or Nigeria.

1.4 How accurate are the figures?

These numbers give an appearance of precision – this is not entirely justified. The long-promised e-Borders system begun as long ago as 2003 is not yet fully operational. By September 2015, the Department

Table 1.1: Summary of the sources of population increase in the year ending 30 June 2016[4]

	Total 2016	Per day
Migration from:		
EU		
Arrivals	284,000	778
Departures	95,000	(260)
Net Increase	189,000	518
Other countries		
Arrivals	289,000	792
Departures	93,000	(255)
Net Increase	196,000	537
UK Citizens		
Returning UK citizens	77,000	211
Departing UK citizens[a]	127,000	(348)
Net decrease	−50,0000	(−137)
Net migration	**335,000**	**920**
Natural Increase (excess of births over deaths)	**193,000**	**529**
Increase in armed forces	9,500	26
Population Increase	**538,500**	**1,475**

[a] It is also worth noting that this category would include those going to work oversees temporarily as well as those retiring permanently to countries such as Spain, Australia, Jamaica or Nigeria.

was collecting data on 86% of those travelling to and leaving the UK, still short of the target it was supposed to have delivered in 2010.[5] So exactly what is happening is still far from clear. For example, there are those who argue that a proportion of students who come here for study then go on to temporary work (permitted under their visas), but then slowly morph into permanent full time work and subsequently become permanent members of our population. For example, according to the ONS's report entitled 'International Student Migration – What do the statistics tell us', in 2014, 75,000 were granted an extension of stay in the UK to study. Of these, 63,000 were granted to former students and the remaining 12,000 were granted to those previously in non-study categories. By contrast in 2013 a total of 219,000 student visas were issued so that when 75,000 were extended in 2014, effectively one in three student visas from 2013 were being extended.[6] The Home Office study, *The Migrant Journey Fifth Report,* published in 2015 showed that 21% of the students who arrived in 2004 still had leave to remain in 2009.[7] Is it realistic to believe that all these truly remain 'students'?

Furthermore, many of the figures given are based on extrapolations of surveys – themselves quite small and completed voluntarily. For example, the International Passenger Survey carried out by the ONS underpins official statistics on migration and is based on sample surveys that collect information from passengers as they leave or enter the UK. They are also statements of intent – on arrival the individual may genuinely expect that he will become, say, a plumber in Hull but in the event may follow a different career in a different part of the country. More significantly, someone intending on arrival merely to visit or to undertake seasonal work might well discover that they can actually get a permanent job with somewhere to live and so choose to stay.

A final source of confusion is that the ONS revise the basis for the collection of figures from time to time – particularly after the ten-yearly censuses – to reflect changing social/economic conditions. As a result current and historic figures do not always match neatly.

Examining the data on the issue of National Insurance numbers (NINOs) enables some form of cross check of numbers entering the UK. Babies born to parents resident in the UK are issued with a NINO when their birth is registered. But for individuals coming from overseas a NINO is essential – it is needed to obtain lawful work, to obtain access to the National Health Service and social security systems as well as for certain tax purposes – and it is also legally required.

The ONS Quarterly Migration Statistics Report for August 2016 revealed that, in the year ending June 2016, 825,000 new NINOs had been issued to individuals from overseas – a decrease of 10% over the previous year.[8] Two nationalities accounted for over one quarter of this figure (Romanians 185,000 and Poles 105,000). Gross immigration in the year ending June 2016 was 650,000. So, the figure for NINOs issued is about 21% higher than the level of reported gross immigration. While one would not expect there to be a complete match, a difference of 175,000 must leave an impression that the actual figures for our total population are higher than reported.

The official answer to this difference is that immigration from the EU has a high level of turnover – individuals who come here for a short term specific role, for example summer fruit picking. While this 'revolving door' may reduce some of the costs to the host state it does not eliminate them entirely (for example healthcare costs). Also, a person is only issued with a National Insurance number once – if you return as a seasonal worker for a second or further years your original number will continue to be of use. So, if this official explanation is true, it means that in the year ending June 2016 175,000 individuals came to carry out temporary work, who had never worked before in this country and were in addition to those who immigrated on a more permanent basis.

1.5 'Zero migration' and 'zero net migration'

It is easy for the layman to be led to believe that, because these two terms sound similar that consequences are the same – in reality their impacts can be dramatically different. 'Zero migration' means nobody comes into and nobody goes out of the UK – an unlikely, and indeed undesirable, situation. 'Zero net migration' means that for every person arriving another person leaves, so that, in the short term, the population is unchanged. But the longer-term impact depends on who is leaving and who is arriving.

It is broadly accepted that emigrants tend to be older and immigrants tend to be younger. Consider the following example. A person retiring decides that he or she wants to live in a warmer climate and so emigrates to live with family in, say, Australia or Jamaica. Meanwhile the immigrant is a plumber from an Eastern European member country of the EU who consequently has a right to free movement to the UK as a worker. The emigrant is no longer a cost to the NHS while the plumber gets a job and pays taxes (this assumes that he does not put a member of the settled population of plumbers out of work). So far, the UK has benefitted. Expenditure on the NHS has been reduced and tax revenues have risen. The emigrant enjoys life in Australia. The plumber works hard and does well. So, after a couple of years he calls up his girlfriend in his home country and suggests she joins him in the UK which, of course, she too is entitled to do under EU freedom of movement. She does and they have a couple of children.

Now the economics for the UK are different. The children quite properly need access to healthcare and education. But more importantly what began as a one for one exchange has over four or five years become one for four and the UK's population is increased by three.

Further, for reasons that are not fully understood the UK appears to be an attractive place to start and bring up a family. As an example, the total fertility rate (TFR) for Polish women in Poland in 2014 was 1.32[9] children – in line with the average Polish TFR over the period 2004-2012 of 1.4.[10] However, for Polish women in the UK in 2011 it was 2.13 children.[11] Similar statistics exist for other Eastern European countries. The overall impact of this higher TFR is shown by the fact that, in 2011, of the 724,000 births in the UK, 185,000 births (25.5%) were to women born *outside* the UK (up from 16.5% ten years ago) while 539,000 births (74%) were to women born in the UK.[12]

The impact of this on the UK's level of natural population increase can be seen in that, as those women become part of the settled population, there is a resulting increase in the UK's TFR which rose from 1.56 to 1.84 – thus narrowing the gap with the TFR of foreign-born mothers which remained constant at 2.2 over the same period. Overall the TFR was 1.84 for women born in the UK and 2.21 for women born outside the UK.[13]

For a shorter period (2001-7) for the UK as a whole some demographers have suggested that foreign-born women contribute 65% of the total increase in the number of births.[14]

This 'second stage' impact of young immigrants is therefore a major cause of the rise in the 'natural increase' component of (47% in 2014) our population. The Migration Observatory at Oxford University suggests that 21% of the natural increase expected in the years to 2035 will be an indirect result of immigration during the 25-year period until 2039.[15]

1.6 The impact of population growth on age structure

As our population grows its immediate numerical impact can be observed both by age structure (the proportion of population in each age range) and the density (by country and region of the UK).

Demographers set out the chronological make-up of a country's population by using a pyramid diagram – a decade for each line with males to the left and females to the right. Figure 1.1 shows what the and

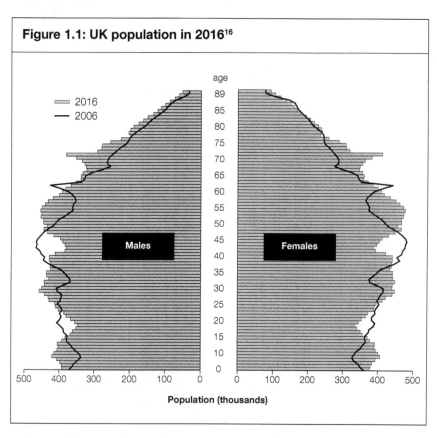

Figure 1.1: UK population in 2016[16]

As can be seen from Figure 1.1 there is a bulge in the age range 45-55 and a slightly smaller one in the age 20-30. The first bulge will present an economic and social challenge in about 10-20 years' time from now as that group begins to retire. However, that challenge may be partly delayed by the continuing economic activity of the group as retirement will occur later following the planned increase in the state pension age from 65 to 68 by 2028. Individuals may

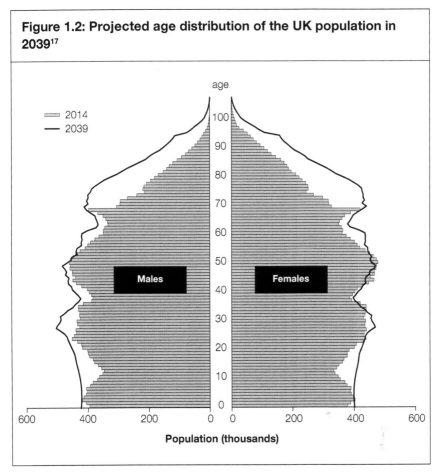

Figure 1.2: Projected age distribution of the UK population in 2039[17]

also decide to continue to be economically active, either to give themselves a continuing practical activity or because there is an economic imperative as a result of not having saved enough in earlier life to afford a sufficiently comfortable retirement.

Figure 1.2 shows two significant trends. First, that in 2039 at almost every age range the population is going to be greater than it is today. Secondly, the increase is particularly significant from ages 70 onwards.

This balance between the economically active and inactive is defined in a statistical measurement called the dependency ratio to which we shall return later.

1.7 Population density for different parts of the UK

The second important consequence of any increase in population is on absolute numbers as well as relative densities (people per sq. km). The latest figures are as follows.

Table 1.2: Population and population densities of UK countries and regions, mid-2015[18]

	Absolute numbers (000's)	Density (people per sq. km)
Scotland	5,373	69
Northern Ireland	1,851	136
Wales	3,099	149
England		
North East	2,624	306
North West	7,173	509
Yorkshire and Humber	5,390	350
East Midlands	4,677	299
West Midlands	5,751	442
East	6,076	318
London	8,673	5,518
South East	8,947	469
South West	5,471	230
Total	54,786	420
Total	65,110	268

What is the impact of population density on issues like social cohesion? Clearly people can and do live successfully in very densely populated conditions such as in city states like Singapore and Monaco. But it is far from clear whether, over the longer term, the members of a society where population growth derives to a significant measure from the arrival of new residents from multiple different backgrounds will co-exist easily unless the settled population feels it has access to a sufficiency of physical space as well as other non-economic resources. They will also wish to be able to reassure themselves that the allocation of such resources has been fairly made. What is of interest is how these densities have changed over the past 25 years.

These figures demonstrate the extent to which, over the past twenty years, the focus of population growth has been in the Southern and Eastern parts of England. The implications of this if it were to continue are discussed in a later chapter.

Table 1.3: Population densities in 1990 and 2015[19]

	(People per sq. km)		% Increase
	1990	2015	
Scotland	65	69	6.2
Northern Ireland	118	136	15.3
Wales	138	149	8.0
England			
North East	301	306	1.7
North West	484	509	5.2
Yorkshire and Humber	319	350	9.1
East Midlands	256	299	16.8
West Midlands	401	442	10.2
East	266	318	19.5
London	4,325	5,518	27.6
South East	398	469	17.8
South West	196	230	17.3
Total England	366	420	13.9
Overall	236	268	12.7

1.8 How does the UK compare with other EU countries?

Another important question is whether the UK's experience of change has been paralleled by other EU countries or whether the UK is an outlier. According to the ONS, 'The population of the UK grew by more than any other EU member state in the year to mid-2013, and at a faster rate than the total EU. From the top ten largest population increases in the year, only Sweden had a higher growth rate than the UK'.[20] The full figures are given in Appendix I (Tables I.2, I.3, I.4 and I.5).

Two conclusions stand out. First, the UK (and particularly England) is far more densely populated than France or Germany. In 2015, the UK had an overall population density of 269 people per sq. km – the equivalent figure for England alone was 420 people – whereas France and Germany had densities of 105 and 229 people per sq. km respectively.

The second important conclusion is seen in the rate of population increase. The UK's rate of population increase is higher than France or Germany – save only for the latter in 2016 no doubt reflecting the high rate of immigration which has caused considerable tension in that country.

As we noted in the last section, population growth is not just about an increase in absolute numbers but also about the resulting population density. From these figures, it is clear that not only is the UK's population growing faster than France's or Germany's but it already has a population density greater than both.

2

How did we get to where we are?

In the previous chapter, we analysed the make-up of the UK's population growth in its two constituent parts – the natural increase (the excess of births over deaths measured by the fertility rate) and net immigration (arrivals less departures) and the balance between. We also noted that the UK's population is growing faster and living in more dense conditions than other EU states. Are these long-term trends?

2.1 The position until 1995

Until the mid-1990s the UK's fertility rates were falling. As a result, the natural increase in the population was low.

Table 2.1: Fertility rates 1960-1995[1]					
	1960	1970	1980	1990	1995
Total fertility rates (TFR)	2.73	2.44	1.90	1.83	1.71

During the same period net immigration remained low. Indeed, there were those in the 1970s and 1980s who argued that the country faced a demographic meltdown.

Table 2.2: Immigration and emigration 1970-1995[2]				
	1970	1980	1990	1995
Immigration	226,000	173,000	267,000	312,000
Emigration	291,000	228,000	231,000	236,000
Net Immigration (Emigration)	(65,000)	(55,000)	36,000	76,000

The result of these two trends was that the population of the UK rose only slowly over about 30 years.

Table 2.3: UK population growth 1960-1995[3]

	1960[4]	1970	1980	1990	1995
UK population (in millions)	52.4	55.6	56.3	57.2	58.0

2.2 Impact of recent policy changes

These trends were changed by two factors. The first was the decision by the Labour Government after coming to power in 1997 to encourage large-scale immigration from the Commonwealth – particularly the new Commonwealth countries of India and Pakistan. Once again, a detailed analysis of underlying trends and impacts is impeded by inadequate data. Not until 2004 was the data collected appropriately. The second was the enlargement of the EU with the admission of the countries of Eastern Europe. Politically

Table 2.4: Summary of the UK's migration data from 1995-2015[5]

	1995	2000	2005	2010	2015
Natural Increase[6]	90,170	68,450	139,585	245,605	171,800
Migration from:					
EU					
Arrivals	61,000	63,000	152,000	176,000	269,000
Departures	38,000	57,000	56,000	99,000	86,000
Net Arrivals	23,000	6,000	96,000	77,000	183,000
Other					
Arrivals	167,000	316,000	317,000	322,000	279,000
Departures	63,000	103,000	119,000	104,000	90,000
Net Arrivals	104,000	213,000	198,000	218,000	189,000
British					
Returning	84,000	99,000	98,000	93,000	84,000
Departing	135,000	161,000	186,000	136,000	124,000
Net departures	–51,000	–62,000	–88,000	–43,000	–40,000
Total Immigration	312,000	479,000	567,000	591,000	631,000
Total Emigration	(236,000)	(321,000)	(361,000)	(339,000)	(299,000)
Net Migration	76,000	158,000	267,000*	256,000*	332,000
Increase in Population	166,170	226,450	406,585	501,605	503,800

*Although the net migration figure does not fit the number created by taking away emigration from immigration these are the figures provided by the ONS.

this may have been an important step to help create a series of stable prosperous societies. But it did mean that for the first time wage disparities within the EU (in which free movement of labour is a founding principle) became sufficiently large to encourage large-scale migration.

Table 2.4 shows the impact. These figures are a summary of the more detailed Table I.6 in Appendix I.

To summarise, over the twenty years 1995-2015 the rate of *natural increase* roughly doubled to 170,000, *net EU migration* rose from 23,000 to 183,000, *net migration from other countries* doubled from 104,000 to just below 200,000 and the net *rate of emigration* of the settled British population remained constant at an annual outflow of around 50,000. During the same period the fertility rate for the country as a whole, which had begun to fall in the 1990s, began to rise again.

Table 2.5: Fertility rate 1990-2015[7]						
	1990	1995	2000	2005	2010	2015
Total fertility rate (TFR)	1.83	1.71	1.64	1.76	1.92	1.81

Overall the evidence suggests that the total fertility rate (TFR) among the settled population is continuing to fall slowly – at the very least, it is not rising. So, as noted earlier, this trend in the TFR appears to be a consequence of the immigration of younger women of child-bearing age who, for the first generation at least, have a higher TFR. In 2013 women born in four countries – Poland, Pakistan, India and Bangladesh – accounted for 8.8% of all the births in the UK.

One critical question for the future rate of increase of the UK population is the extent to which the higher TFR for foreign-born mothers persists in subsequent generations. And if the TFR drops closer to the average for the larger settled population, how quickly it does so.

3

Future levels of UK population

So, what lies ahead? The uncertainties of the future lie heavy on the demographer. Quite small changes in underlying factors – such as the total fertility rate (TFR) or life expectancy – cumulatively have a significant impact over time.

For example, a Government White Paper in 1972 expressed concern that the population of the UK might reach 65.6m by 2011 – in fact the actual figure was 63.2m.[1] Even over shorter periods the differences can be quite significant.

3.1 What are the estimates?

The Government Actuary's Department/Office of National Statistics (ONS) provides a series of predictions as follows.

Table 3.1: ONS population projections (in millions)[2]								
	2014	2020	2025	2030	2035	2039	2050	2080
High (High Population)	–	68.0	70.9	73.9	76.8	79.1	*	*
Principal	64.6	67.8	69.4	71.4	73.0	74.3	77.7	85.7
Low (Low Population)	–	66.6	67.8	68.6	69.1	69.3	*	*

*The ONS does not produce varied projections beyond 2039

The difference between the projections results from making different assumptions about the age at which people die, about the number of children each woman has (the fertility rate), the level of net immigration and the interplay between the latter two.

What is interesting is that ONS projections in recent years on the likely rate of population growth have consistently underestimated the rate of growth. For example, in November 2001 the Government Actuary Office, using the 2000 population data, estimated the UK population in 2011 to be 61.9m[3] – in fact it was 63.2m. Looking further ahead, the 2001 projections by the Government Actuary Office estimated a population of 65.6m for 2031 whereas the 2014 population-based projections now estimate the UK population will be 71.3m in 2031, an underestimation of more than 6m people. And the principal projection of the UK's population in 2024 is now 249,000 higher than that made 12 months ago.

The key underlying assumptions of the current principal projections are that:

(i)   Life expectancy rises from 79.1 for males and 82.8[4] for females in the current figures available, to 84.1 for males and 86.9 for females in 2039.[5]

(ii)   Net immigration falls from 336,000 today to 185,000[6] in 2039.

(iii) The UK's total fertility rate rises from 1.81 to 1.89 over the same period.

3.2 What are the consequences?

If one accepts these assumptions as given the consequences are as follows.

A. Overall[7]

(i)   Under the principal projection, the UK population is projected to increase from an estimated 64.6m as of June 2014 by 4.4m over the next 10 years reaching 69.0m in 2024 and by 9.7m over the next 25 years reaching 74.3m in mid-2039. The 70m figure will be reached in mid-2027.

(ii)   Net migration will account for 51% of the projected increase over the next 25 years, with natural increase (more births than deaths) accounting for the remaining 49% of growth.

B. Age distribution

(i)   The population is projected to continue ageing, with the average (median) age rising from 40.0 years in 2014 to 40.9 years in mid-2024 and 42.9 by mid-2039.

(ii)   By mid-2039, more than one in twelve of the population is projected to be aged 80 or over – almost double the current figure. The number of centenarians is projected to rise nearly six-fold, from 14,000 in 2014 to 83,000 in 2039.[8]

C. Population density

(i) The population density of the UK is projected to increase from 268 people per sq. km (mid-2015)[9] to be 305 in 2039.[10] At the 'high' projection this figure will reach 325.[11]

(ii) The population density of England alone is projected to increase from 420 people per sq. km in mid-2015 to 486 in 2039.[12] At the 'high' projection this figure will reach 515.[13] This will make England more densely populated than current day Netherlands.

3.3 What is projected elsewhere in the EU?

What makes these figures even starker is to compare them with the projections for France and Germany. (The detailed figures are shown in Appendix I, Tables I.7 and I.8.) Again clear trends emerge.

First, today the UK has a population of 64.9m – slightly below that of France (66.4m) and well below that of Germany (81.2m). By contrast over the period to 2080 the UK's population is expected to grow by 27% (Germany's will decline by 4.2% and France's increase by 18.3%). As a consequence by 2080 the UK will have overtaken Germany as the most populous country in Europe (82.4m against 79.2m).

Second, there is a parallel consequence in population densities. The UK's population density will reach 332 people per sq. km. (England alone is estimated to be 532).[14] So, by 2080 the UK will be 1.5 times as densely populated as Germany and 2.7 times as densely populated as France. One can broadly forecast that England alone in 2050 will have a population density of 484 persons per sq. km,[15] almost twice that of Germany and four times that of France.

4

Implications for our communities

If we accept the ONS assumptions underlying their principal projection, including that net migration will fall considerably from present levels, we must nevertheless expect an additional 9.7m residents of the UK over the next 25 years. If one believes that migration will continue at present levels the population will be 2-3m higher still.

What does 9.7m people look like? Using ONS 2015 figures the current population of Greater Manchester is 2.8m, that of the West Midlands conurbation is 5.8m.[1] So, we are going to have to build new towns equivalent to 3.5 times that of Greater Manchester or 1.7 times that of the West Midlands conurbation.

So much for the national numbers. The national numbers tell a story but they are so large as to seem remote, impersonal and indeed incomprehensible. Nevertheless, however incomprehensible these national figures may be they will have a knock-on impact on every individual community. The new arrivals will need houses, schools, doctors, jobs and leisure facilities.

One can make the likely impact more comprehensible if one draws assumptions about what might happen in specific parts of the country if the projections of previous chapters come about and the distribution of population remains broadly the same.

Clearly it is not possible to forecast exactly where these additional 9.7m residents will end up living. Some may argue that any forecasts are worthless. But there are good reasons why, over the short term at least, the distribution might well not change significantly. This is for two main reasons.

4.1 Friction of distance

Some argue that as the disadvantages (housing costs etc) of living and working in the South East increase there will be a natural tendency to move to other parts of the country. There is undoubtedly some truth in that assertion though it could be argued that it is somewhat perverse to have policies which result in the settled population finding themselves forced to leave their capital city and its surrounding region.

But it ignores what economists call 'the friction of distance'. This is based on the notion that to overcome distance requires the expenditure of effort, energy and/or money (for example, the commuter's season ticket or the time taken travelling to and from work every day).

While technology (such as email and telephone conferencing) is facilitating the dispersal of jobs there are a whole series of activities that cannot be dispersed – the man who empties the dustbins, the nurse in the hospital, or the policeman on the beat. Such people, often working shifts and not enormously well paid, simply cannot afford to live too far away from their place of work.

HS2 is an example of a valiant attempt to reduce the friction of distance but it is likely to be of assistance primarily to senior and middle managers, not waiters in restaurants.

4.2 Centripetal force of London and the South East

While London and the South East may have a high cost of living there are multiple reasons which compensate for this.

Of course, some of them are straight-forwardly economic – salary levels, bonus opportunities etc. But no less important is the longer-term potential for career development. Ambitious people, particularly young people, see London and the South East with its concentration of commercial, professional and creative activity as the area in which they are most likely to be able to achieve rapid career advancement.

But there is also the background of life in London and its appeal – 'the vibe' – the range of cultural, sporting and recreational opportunities. And as more young people come to London they in turn attract others. An article in the *Financial Times* laid out the challenges to the rest of the country in an article about the 'brain drain' that jeopardises efforts to revitalise north.[2]

So, if we accept that dramatic short term population shifts are unlikely we can check the historic rate of population growth for each of four very different communities and make an extrapolation as to what an additional 9.7m people over the next quarter century distributed across the country in roughly similar proportions might mean for each of them.

The four communities are in different parts of the UK and have very different history and prospects.

1. Dundee

Based on the Tay estuary, Dundee was once the centre of the jute industry. The collapse of the industry during the 20th century, partly due to reduced demand for jute products and partly due to an inability to compete with the emerging industry in India, contributed to slowing of Dundee's economy which has struggled to find alternative employment.

2. Stockton-on-Tees

In the heart of the North East, Stockton-on-Tees suffered severely from the rundown of heavy industry. In recent years, the opening of a campus of Durham University has helped to begin its regeneration along with large investment in its waterfront.

3. Norwich

A cathedral city with an established, well-respected university. It is relatively isolated in East Anglia and remains outside easy commuting distance from London. It is reliant on agriculture and the university and is in need of improving infrastructure to keep pace with other parts of England

4. Guildford

Also a cathedral city, Guildford is in the heart of the South Eastern commuter belt. Becoming more prosperous as London grows, Guildford and the surrounding area is becoming a key hub for the South of England. It includes the Hogs Back and the Surrey Hills, both Areas of Outstanding Natural Beauty.

Analysing in detail the consequences of population growth is made difficult by the variety of projections made by different local and national bodies.

The ONS and National Records of Scotland (NRS) provide a regional breakdown of their 2014-based population projections. Using this and previous census data one can plot the trend of population growth throughout our communities.

Table 4.1: Population projections for selected councils[3]					
	1991	2001	2011	2039 (est.)	Expected increase 2011- 2039
Dundee	149,200	145,700	147,300	156,900[4]	9,600
Norwich	120,900	122,400	132,500	161,000	28,500
Stockton-on-Tees	175,300	183,800	191,600	214,000	22,400
Guildford	122,000	129,800	137,200	171,000	33,800

While by no means all of the practical implications of these population increases are easily measurable, there are some that are easier to pick out.

The most easily identifiable is the need for additional housing. The Government provides household projections for local authority districts up until 2039 based on ONS data. The NRS also provide household projections for local authority districts up until 2039.

Because each council prepares a local plan one can then cross-check to see in reality how many houses each council is planning to build. The figures are as shown in Table 4.2.

4.3 What it might mean for Dundee, Stockton-On-Tees, Norwich and Guildford

So, on the basis of the Government figures, Norwich and Guildford will have to build about 1.4 houses per day for the next 25 years, Stockton about 1.2 per day and Dundee just less then one a day.

For those who do not accept that the present distribution of population will continue it is nevertheless unanswerable that our increasing population is going to have to live somewhere, so some local authority somewhere is going to have to allow these houses to be built. What is not clear is the extent to which housebuilders

Table 4.2: Comparison of projected housing need (number of homes needed) and actual plans by selected local councils

	Projected Housing Need[5(a)]		Local Authority Local Plan[(b)]	
	Total 2014-2039	Per annum 2014-2039	Total	Per annum
Dundee	7,500[6]	300	5,800 2016-2028[7]	411
Norwich	13,000	520	19,900 2012-2036[8]	830
Stockton-on-Tees	11,000	440	9,100 2017-2032[9]	607
Guildford	13,000	520	10,900 2015-2034[10]	574

[(a)] Projected housing need is based on broad projections from the ONS and the NRS.
[(b)] Local plans are provided by corresponding councils. They differ from the ONS/NRS figures because a council-produced Strategic Housing Market Assessment uses both ONS projections and predicted economic growth.

already hold land banks with associated planning permissions and how many houses are potentially therefore 'in the pipeline'. There is also the question as to how much land is available on 'brownfield' sites – past industrial sites – or land held by the government. In response to Written Parliamentary Question HL 31 asked on 21 June 2017, on the extent of 'brownfield land', the Government explained that 'up-to-date information on brownfield land is not currently available. Legislation to require local authorities to publish registers of brownfield land suitable for housing by 31st December 2017 came into force on 16 April 2017.'

But of course, housing is only the beginning of the demands – both spatial and financial – that any increase in population will make. A proportion of the new population will require jobs, so additional factories or offices will have to be built; they will need to be able to travel reasonably quickly and smoothly between their home and place of employment, so additional roads and maybe railways will need to be constructed. Their children will need access to schools and the schools will need teachers. They will all need healthcare facilities (GP surgeries, additional hospital capacity) again with doctors, nurses, ambulance crews and others to run them. They will expect the huge support network demanded by modern society – not just critical support functions like the police and fire services but other 'softer' resources such as social services and leisure facilities (swimming pools, football pitches, running tracks etc).

So, what might these housing figures mean in terms of additional land usage? Currently the government suggests a *net* residential density of 30-50 houses per hectare (12-20 houses per acre). Recent developments across the country have averaged 42 houses per hectare (17 houses per acre). But *net* residential activity refers only to the actual house and gardens and maybe half the width of the required access road. *Gross* residential density provides an allowance for the provision of certain services and amenities, e.g. schools and parks. But a further allowance needs to be made for linked economic activity – additional shops, offices, factories and associated access roads.

A final complication is that every council's land usage will vary depending on its own planned housing mix – the number of flats, sheltered housing, starter homes etc. And whether any associated economic activity falls within its own council's area.

So, while it is possible to be fairly precise about likely *net* residential densities, this does not hold true for *gross* residential density and still less so for the space required for associated economic activity.

Some planners have suggested that an additional 20-25% space over net residential density would be needed to give adequate open and recreational space. On top of that there would need to be a pro rata share of the space needed for additional educational and health facilities. Finally, there is the space required for associated economic activity – shops, factories, warehouses, offices and required communication links.

Data on these space calculations is hard to find but an add-on of 75-100% to *net* residential density does seem reasonable. So, while net residential density targets 17 houses per acre the gross density after making allowance for the additional space requirements is likely to be half that – effectively eight houses per acre.

Using the two sets of figures, one from the ONS/NRS and the other from the local authority's own plan – the people of Guildford must expect to see 65-70 acres lost to development in each of the years up to 2039, the people of Norwich, 65-100 acres, of Stockton-on-Tees 55-75 acres and the people of Dundee 40-50.

5

Why increase our population?

What are the strategic arguments deployed for and against population growth?

5.1 Economic advantage

The basic economic case for increasing our population – especially from immigration – can be simply stated. Immigration can result in an injection of skills, dynamism and entrepreneurial flair. It can theoretically raise standards and productivity while encouraging improved performance from our existing workforce. It could fill gaps in our skills which cannot otherwise be found amongst the settled population.

However, while that might well be so in theory, such impacts depend fundamentally on who actually arrives. The economic impact of, say, a group of penniless immigrants from Sub-Saharan Africa who can neither read nor write English will be very different from the impact of a similar number of established Chinese entrepreneurs.

But too often in the past the argument has been based on the value of simply increasing total GDP. That surely is today's glimpse of the obvious. If an increase in population were not to lead to a higher total GDP – it would indeed be a perverse outcome.

It is interesting to note that the assessment carried out for the Commission of the EU taking in 3m refugees suggested a boost of 0.2-0.5% to the EU economy.[1] But closer analysis of the figures showed that this was the result of expenditure (cost to the state) in housing these people and providing them with health, education and social benefits. This expenditure was not 'free' and would have to be paid for either by borrowing or raising taxes so that any short term economic impact might well be cancelled out by longer term disbenefits.

So, a better question is about the impact on GDP *per head*. And not just the immediate GDP per head but over the longer term. In an earlier chapter, we looked at the possible consequences of a zero-net migration policy whereby one emigrant (an older person to the sunshine) is replaced initially by one immigrant (from Eastern Europe) potentially, though not necessarily, giving initially an increase in GDP per head. But after a few years when the latter has been joined by his partner and they have a family the resulting GDP per head may not have increased. As an authoritative cross-party House of Lords study put it:

> Overall GDP, which the Government has persistently emphasised, is an irrelevant and misleading criterion for assessing the economic impacts of immigration on the UK. The total size of an economy is not an index of prosperity. The focus of analysis should rather be on the effects of immigration on income per head of the resident population. Both theory and the available empirical evidence indicate that these effects are small, especially in the long run when the economy fully adjusts to the increased supply of labour. In the long run, the main economic effect of immigration is to enlarge the economy, with relatively small costs and benefits for the incomes of the resident population.[2]

So, the second question is, if there are benefits to whom do they accrue?

First among these is the issue of 'crowding out' – that with unrestricted immigration, from Europe at least, the skills and rights of the settled population can too often be overlooked. The term 'settled population' can appropriately be used as a description of all those living permanently or intending to live permanently in the UK and are legally entitled so to do. Most importantly it avoids the issue of demography being hijacked on grounds of race, religion or colour.

Commentators have begun to note that one of the consequences of our increasing population is the economic 'crowding out' of our 'settled population'. Some have remarked that this has a particularly severe impact on the first and second generations of the settled population.

Examples of crowding out abound. They include football's Premier League. The Premier League is a huge worldwide commercial success and earns millions of dollars for the UK. But, attempting to explain England's poor performance in the last World Cup, the Football Association pointed out that less than 32% of the players in the Premier League are British.[3] Does this matter? In the balance sheet of UK plc probably not. The dreams and aspirations of, say, 500 young men may have to be sacrificed for the economic benefit of the rest of us.

But it is not just about footballers, there is an impact right across swathes of the working population. It can be easier for a fruit grower to ask a gangmaster to provide 100 temporary workers – all of whom incidentally will be issued with a permanent National Insurance number – to undertake fruit picking for a couple of months in the summer than to hire 100 British workers individually. The gangmaster takes responsibility for all the interviewing and associated paperwork before delivering and removing the workers on the agreed dates.

It can be easier and cheaper for UK employers to recruit trained craftsman from Europe as opposed to undertaking the training up of members of the settled population. This may explain in part why businesses so strongly support immigration since it is in at least their short-term economic interest to do so. It is also why the Government plan to create 3m new apprenticeships during the life of this Parliament is so important. It improves the work chances of our settled population and at the same time, reduces pressure to increase population.

It can be easier and cheaper for the National Health Service to recruit doctors and nurses from all over the world, even from less developed countries, than to expand training programmes for our settled population. In the report permitting increased immigration of healthcare workers, Professor Sir David Metcalfe, Chair of the Migration Advisory Committee, said: 'We have reluctantly made this recommendation. However, there is no good reason why the supply of nurses cannot be sourced domestically, there seems to be an automatic presumption that non-EEA skilled migration provides the health and care sector with a "Get out Jail Free" card'.[4] Though this pamphlet is about the direct impact of population growth on the United Kingdom, one cannot but note the indirect impact on this country of an unstable world. It is hard to see how draining less developed countries of their skilled population (doctors, nurses, engineers, scientists etc) contributes to creating or maintaining stability in those countries.

That is not to argue that there are no cases where overseas recruitment should properly take place. Specialist skills may not be available in the UK. Some recruitment from overseas can refresh and reinvigorate but immigration as the default option can disadvantage our settled population.

Writing in the *Financial Times* on 25 February 2016, in an in-depth article analysing the impact of the Brexit campaign, the paper's economics editor Chris Giles concluded:

> Some aspects of EU membership have not been so good for the British economy. Today one in 20 UK residents was born in another EU country. But numerous studies have shown that most gains from immigration have fallen to the immigrants themselves. Apart from a net benefit to public finances of importing workers, free movement has not itself obviously increased British people's prosperity.[5]

There is one further potentially highly significant economic impact of an 'open door' policy. The Achilles heel of the UK's economic performance has been our poor record of improving productivity. Some evidence has pointed towards a positive relationship between immigration and productivity. For instance, work by the National Institute of Economic and Social Research (NIESR) suggested that 'a 1% increase in the immigrant share in the labour force is associated with an increase in labour productivity of between 0.06 and 0.07 percent'.[6] However, despite continuing high rates of net migration our productivity has not significantly risen. Today the UK still has the third lowest productivity in the G7 and as the Financial Times argued, 'productivity growth has been the missing part of the recovery since 2009 with output per hour worked and output per job barely higher than at the peak in 2007'.[7] Clearly, unrestricted immigration is not leading to a growth in productivity. That is because, ultimately, as the

Migration Observatory argues, 'the impacts of immigration on the labour market critically depend on the skills of migrants'.[8] In a letter to *The Times* on 23 June 2017 Professor George Rzevksi, Emeritus Professor of Complexity Science at the Open University, wrote:

> ...if you tighten up employment law and make it more difficult for businesses to employ cheap immigrant labour... business would adapt and start investing in IT and switch from labour-intensive to technology-driven, high-productivity businesses processes.[9]

He went on to suggest that France's more restrictive employment laws may be one of the reasons why France's productivity record is better than the UK's.

5.2 Dangers of an imbalanced population

The second broad argument in favour of a growing population is to avoid any imbalance in our population. Each of us begins and ends our individual lives consuming more than our average share of the resources of the state – in our early years on healthcare and education and in our later years on health and social care. In between, during our working lives as taxpayers most will pay more to the state than we consume.

This ratio of young and old on the one hand and those in work on the other is an important element in achieving a financial balance for the nation as a whole. It is expressed arithmetically as the proportion of dependants (younger than 15 or older than 64) per 100 of the working age population – the 'dependency ratio'.

It will be realised immediately that there are two completely separate dependent proportions of the population – young and old – so it is helpful to look at the two figures separately.

Table 5.1: UK dependency ratio 1960 (projected figures for 2040)[10]

UK Dependency Ratio	1960	1980	2000	2015	2025	2040
Old	18.10	23.40	24.40	28.20	32.50	40.70
Young	35.60	32.80	29.30	27.40	28.40	27.10
Total	53.60	56.20	53.70	55.50	60.90	67.80

The message is stark and clear – not only is the overall dependency ratio rising but the proportions are shifting dramatically as the population of the UK ages.

So, the argument runs, we need to increase our working age population both to provide the tax revenue needed to fund the state generally and, in particular, health and social care required by the elderly and additionally as to provide the man/womanpower to carry out the actual physical work providing care for the increasingly elderly population.

But one has to be careful not to use historic methods of measurement which may have become less relevant. As noted the definition of the dependency ratio is those aged 65 or above. This has historically been the age of retirement. But this is no longer the case; the UK's retirement age will rise to 68 by 2025. As people live longer and are healthier they will wish, or may have, to work longer. Analysis will show that increasing the definition of old age for the purpose of the dependency ratio from 65 to 68 has a dramatic effect on the actual ratio. For example, a person who joins the workforce today will likely have an increase in their working life of not far short of 10%.

Second, we need to consider the impact of technology. The cost (both financial and operational) of social care is that it is manpower intensive, requiring physical visits to individuals in their homes. To reduce these costs people are urged/forced to move into specially designed facilities. Not only are these facilities expensive to build but many people would prefer to stay in their own family home for longer. That is where technology should be able to help. There are a growing number of affordable electronic systems (pressure pads and electronic beams) which can monitor people more closely and more sensitively (both in their own house and in special facilities). As a result, the manpower required may well be dramatically reduced.

Finally, we need to remember the undeniable rule that we all age. Today's young people will become tomorrow's old people. And, of course, as they age they will in turn require yet more young people to look after them. This will require yet further increases in our population so accentuating the challenges outlined in this pamphlet, as a result of what Sir David Attenborough memorably has called a 'Population Ponzi Scheme'.[11]

In a speech at the London School of Economics in 2007, Adair Turner showed that if we sought to maintain the then current dependency ratio the UK would need 27.4m more workers by 2050 which will take the UK population to over 100m compared to the current estimate of 78m: a 30% increase over the current mid projection and a 50% increase over the latest ONS population estimate of 65.6m.[12]

5.3 Quality of life

A strategic argument against population growth is that viewing the issue solely through an economic prism fails to recognise that there are other important societal consequences. 'Crowding out' is not just about the economic prospects of the low paid it also has 'quality of life' implications – 'externalities' in economist speak.

Consider the property market in London and the South East. The UK has been a magnet for foreign property investment from all over the world. Why is this? No doubt the apparently inexorable rise in prices over the past decade is a great attraction. But the attraction of our stable society can surely be no less significant. For at least three centuries property rights in the UK have been sacrosanct and the country has benefited from a rule of law free of political bias and interference. So, if you live in a country which does not have these advantages where better to invest money than in a UK property – it provides the triple advantages of a 'legally safe' purchase, a bolthole if events drive you from your own home country as well as an asset which, in recent years at least, has risen steadily in value. The consequence is in the many reports in recent years of several London property developments being sold 'off plan' and a large number of properties particularly in central London only lived in for a relatively short time in any year if at all.[13]

As London house prices rise, similar impacts are being seen elsewhere in the UK. An article in *The Times* showed that a development in Manchester of 300 flats had attracted buyers from 18 different countries and that only 17 flats were sold to UK buyers.[14]

Now, there is much to be welcomed in this development – money flowing into the country, employment (though probably for the most part at a relatively low-paid level of drivers, cleaners, domestic staff) being created – what's not to like?

But the very conditions that have led to this are the consequence of the behaviour of the settled population over the past three centuries. So, the respect shown by the settled population for the rule of law and property rights have tipped 'the terms of trade' against them making London property unaffordable to all but a handful of the settled population. A further consequence is that the ripples spread ever wider across the South East. For example, according to the Lloyds Bank Affordable Cities Review, Oxford is now the most expensive city after London with an average price of £365,000 being 11 times the average gross annual earnings in the city.[15] Thus, an increasing proportion of the young/settled population living, or seeking to live, in the South East have found themselves unable to get onto the property ladder. Accordingly, they are having either to continue to live with their parents, to rent at the expense of an increasingly large proportion of their salaries or to accept longer periods and higher costs to travel to work.

London and the South East is a special case. But if by 2039 we are going to build the 4.2m additional houses needed as suggested by our projected population these stresses must surely be repeated more widely across the country. The Manchester example given above may well be a precursor.

Part of the housing challenge is not just about availability and price, it is about environment. Many individuals, at every level of society, wish to buy a home – in many cases the single most significant financial transaction of their lives – and do so in anticipation of a reasonably stable environment around their home. When they are subsequently told that future development plans will transform that environment they are resentful. Some – usually those who are in a position not so affected – may decry this is as selfish Nimbyism. Others accept the argument that people are entitled to object vigorously to proposals which may affect the value – looked at in the broadest sense – of the home which very often they will have scrimped and saved for years to acquire.

There is no financial accounting that can measure environmental change or degradation of this sort. But an inability to measure does not make it any less real to those who experience such changes, so there is a danger that this may loosen the ties that bind our society together. One has only to consider the public reaction to the proposed HS2 line or the new runway for Heathrow Airport to see what may lie ahead over the next 25 years.

5.4 Social contract

A contract, unspoken and unwritten, underpins many aspects of our society. The acceptance of this contract by everyone of us provides, inter alia, a National Health Service, free at the point of delivery which accounted for 18.8% (£145bn) of total government expenditure in the 2016 Budget,[16] a pay-as-you-go pension scheme which results in the national scheme which some estimate as being underfunded by some £2.3 trillion;[17] and a largely non-contributory social security system which costs £240bn per annum.[18]

No-one willingly pays taxes. So how is it that these enormous sums can be raised year after year? One can argue that the principal reason is that the population as a whole believe them to be 'fair'. The British people place great weight on fairness.

But 'fairness' is not just about money. It has a qualitative element. It underpins the readiness of the British public as a whole to provide a refuge to some arrivals from less fortunate lands. Or acceptance that some environmental change in the local neighbourhood is inevitable. But in reaching a conclusion as to what is 'fair' each one of us wants to be reassured of an appropriate degree of transparency of the overall cost of population increases – for example assimilation costs in the education system or future liabilities of the NHS.

So, there is a balance to be struck between rich and poor, young and old, working and not working, advantaged and disadvantaged, individuals who have been here for generations and people who have arrived only recently.

Fairness is an elusive concept and one which undoubtedly changes depending on the eye of the beholder. But it is at root a concept which have motivated the population as a whole to accept decisions which have not gone in their favour or policies which have not been to their advantage.

Fairness is also an elastic concept, but not infinitely, so one cannot forecast what, if anything may cause the elastic to fray and snap. But changes to our society of the magnitude likely to result from the projected increase in our population suggest that this is not an issue to be ignored or passed over lightly.

5.5 Skills and attitude 'gaps'

Challenges to our social cohesion will be most acutely felt at lower wage levels in the more disadvantaged parts of the country. We have already discussed the 'skills gap' – that because of wage differentials in other parts of the EU and world it makes economic sense for an employer to take on a more skilled person from outside the UK, particularly if they will accept, a lower skilled and lower paid job in the UK. But whatever the rational economic argument for these behaviours it ignores the consequent impact on members of the settled population who may see their way of life (in the broadest sense) under threat. And not just their way of life but equally important the way of life for their children. It is facile to call such people 'racist' or 'xenophobic' – not least because there are strong arguments that those communities that will be most affected by any breakdown in social cohesion will be those made up of the more disadvantaged or more recently arrived sections of the population.

Those members of the settled population who have lived in the UK for some period of time have inbuilt advantages of knowing quite unconsciously how society 'works' – this knowledge can be very subtle and deployed quite unconsciously – but it does not exist to the same extent amongst the more recently arrived. For them hope and expectation may be followed by disillusionment, apathy and resentment.

Second there may be an 'attitude gap'. People who leave their homes behind to seek their fortune outside their country have by definition shown a degree of drive and ingenuity. It may have required them simply to board a long-distance bus in an Eastern European city or it may have required them to undertake a long and potentially life-threatening trip at the mercy of unscrupulous people smugglers, but whether it results from a wish to seek comparative economic advantage or desperation to escape intolerable living conditions, an element of self-belief is present.

With that self-belief comes an unwillingness to fail – for example, not to go back to their village in Eastern Europe and admit they did not succeed. So, such people are prepared to go the extra mile. This extra mile may include the effort put into their work, the acceptance of poor living conditions (such as semi-dormitory accommodation), or the willingness to tolerate poor pay and working conditions. Some people attribute low rates of wage growth to the result of the economic turbulence since 2008 and there is evidence that pay for at least some sectors of the UK economy has been directly and negatively impacted by the recruitment of individuals from overseas. A paper from the Bank of England concluded 'that the biggest effect is in the semi/unskilled services sector, where a 10-percentage point rise in the proportion of immigrants is associated with a two per cent reduction in pay'.[19]

This 'attitude gap' should not surprise us. Looked at narrowly, why would a member of the settled population want to give up his/her established life with its social, family and other connections in one part of the country to move to another to live in a dormitory?

The concern is that social cohesion may be threatened if a sufficient number or group of the settled population feels that the overall prospects for them and for their families are unduly restricted or threatened.

'Hollowing Out'

A rapidly rising population may well accentuate tensions in society brought about by technological developments.

The revolution in information technology and communications has, inter alia, facilitated the outsourcing of jobs, first to Eastern Europe and then to India, China and the Far East. This has reduced inflationary pressures but has also reduced – some would say stopped – the rate of rise in blue collar living standards. The anger and frustration that this has caused has fuelled the rise of political parties espousing more unconventional policies – for example Donald Trump's US presidential campaign.

But we are about to be hit by a second more potentially serious wave, over the next 5-10 years, resulting from the increasing use of artificial intelligence and robotics. It is argued that wide swathes of jobs in offices and administrative functions are going to disappear. For the first time, middle income families are going to be affected in large numbers. Further it is argued that while earlier phases *created* more jobs than they destroyed, this phase will *destroy* more jobs than it creates.

A rapidly increasing population seems likely to create conditions which will accentuate the bitterness of middle and lower middle income families who may have seen their job security, their future way of life and the future way of life for their children changed irrevocably.

6

Concluding thoughts

The kaleidoscope of concerns about the consequences of changes in the population in this country is constantly shifting. Well publicised past premonitions of disaster – most notably the Club of Rome 1972 report 'Limits to Growth' – proved to have been misplaced.[1] More recently in 2009 some eminent academics were predicting 'a permanent and increasing scarcity of oil'[2] within ten years; now eight years later oil is below $50 a barrel and the problem is oversupply not scarcity.

So as regards future population levels governments of all persuasion have been tempted to follow Albert Einstein's dictum: 'I never think of the future. It comes soon enough.'

But perhaps the preceding chapters have demonstrated that there is enough evidence to suggest that the challenges of greater population are unlikely to melt away over the next quarter century unless one of two things happen – some unforeseen worldwide catastrophe or living standards in various parts of the UK becoming sufficiently stressed and undesirable to make this country unattractive to new arrivals. Neither of these are desirable outcomes!

There are strong arguments that whatever the nature of the population challenge there are steps that the Government could usefully take.

6.1 Creating a strategic policy framework

At the moment, not all government departments take into account population changes as part of their departmental planning. Those that do look only at their individual piece of the population jigsaw. So the Department for Communities and Local Government will consider demand for housing and infrastructure; the Department of Health will consider demands for healthcare etc. This work is paralleled by a number of non-governmental bodies (for example the Migration Advisory Committee).

All of these bodies do valuable work but it is work from the bottom up – reacting to a set of possible scenarios that might or might not reflect the real range of possible outcomes. It appears vanishingly little effort has been made to look at the challenges from the top down and to unravel the tangled threads of claim and counter claim.

To tackle this the Government should appoint a Minister for Demography. That title – rather than Minister for Population – is important in two senses. It insulates the issue from a potentially toxic focus on immigration and race. Secondly it emphasises that the issue is not just about numbers but no less importantly about the *impact* of the numbers on the country as a whole.

Its work would be cross-departmental and its analysis and conclusions would be used to guide and inform the decisions of policy makers generally.

6.2 *Informing the wider debate*

But the role of a Department of Demography needs to reach beyond a solely Whitehall focus to discuss, debate and inform the wider reaches of UK government and society. As noted earlier the primary impact of population change will be felt at a local level. It is at a local level that potential threats to social cohesion can be identified and addressed yet local government either has not chosen or does not have the means to get involved in the debate. The Department should also have a role in introducing the general public to the complexities of this issue:

The Department should undertake research into the interaction of the various impacts of population change – particularly the non-economic ones. Are there points at which population density is likely to pose a threat to social cohesion? What is the overall impact of each one of us – spatially, environmentally and economically? How accurate are the claims and counter-claims of economic benefit? How fairly are the proceeds of this economic benefit, if any, shared?

The objective would be to move the public debate beyond a series of short term localised preoccupations to a wider consideration of what may lie ahead for the country as a whole. In particular, it could draw attention to the implications of changes (up or down) in the UK's total fertility rate (TFR).

As noted earlier the implications of demographic change are generational. The demographic prospects for the country over the next ten or so years to 2025 are now largely set in stone. It is beyond that date that policy decisions taken now will begin to have an impact. In particular, the challenges posed by the inherently exponential (compounding) nature of population – whether rising or falling – are poorly researched or understood. As a simple example, growth of 0.5% per annum over 25 years would result in a population of 65.5m growing to 74.2m but a growth of 1.5% over the same period results in a population of 95m – over 20m higher!

6.3 Learning from other nations

At some point in the future the UK along with all other countries will have to learn to live with a near static, or completely static, population.

When that position will be reached is a matter for debate but that it will happen at some point is inarguable. And the UK, given its small geographic size, is likely to be one of the first major economies to reach this point. Indeed, if the Conservative Government's stated policy of reducing immigration to the 'tens of thousands' from its recent level of more than 300,000 were successful this will lead, over time, to a near static population.

Some other countries, most notably Japan, are already having to face these challenges. In Japan, with a dependency ratio of 64[3] (UK in 2015 had a dependency ratio of 55),[4] today more than half the households include a relative aged over 65.[5]

It would be useful for the development of the UK's demographics policy to examine in some detail the consequent stresses with a view to learning from this experience and better preparing the UK.

6.4 Establishing the evidence base

The work of a Department of Demography will rightly only command public and governmental confidence if its conclusions are properly evidence based.

It would seem that the existing foundations for any evidence base are far from secure. As noted in several places in this report demography is an uncertain science. And even properly researched policy decisions can still reach perverse conclusions; for example, the work on which the Labour Government based its policy decision to have an 'open door' policy as regards workers from the new Eastern European members of the EU was undertaken by serious economists. That report suggested that only 13,000 people would arrive per annum from Eastern Europe, in the event the figure for 2014 was 112,000.[6]

The reasons for a lower level of public confidence include that the evidence is based on small sample passenger surveys which are only completed voluntarily with no subsequent check on veracity; that the procedure for visa extensions is far from clear which leads to a view that, inter alia, many individuals who enter on a student visa morph into the settled population over a number of years; that the anecdotal evidence of stowaways jumping out of container lorries and disappearing is increasing; that there is confusion over the discrepancy between the number of National Insurance numbers (NINOs) being issued and the general level of immigration; finally that 12 years since its inception and at least £830m[7] later the e-Borders system appears still not complete.

But the Government in its various guises has access to a great deal of information on which to base informed policy decisions. The challenge is that it is held in different departmental silos which do not appear to be able to communicate with one another.

In any event there are serious issues here for a Department of Demography to unpick. The present situation is damaging in at least three respects. First any 'leakage' increases the demand for the inevitably limited resources of the state. Second such 'leakage' is unfair to those who have come here legally. Thirdly and most corrosively, it creates and feeds a populist view of the general nature of those seeking to come to this country.

6.5 *The position of Scotland*

Scotland has the lowest density of population in the UK – in part this results from the geography of the country which renders a proportion of it effectively uninhabitable. Population levels/ demography are devolved matters. The Scottish Government has a stated policy of increasing the population of Scotland, matching EU 15 population growth from 2007-2017, a target they are currently beating.[8] The challenge of this is that there is, quite rightly, freedom of movement within the UK – so if the Scottish policy of increasing the country's population is fulfilled by encouraging higher immigration there is nothing to stop those arrivals heading south at any time and so accentuating the challenge to England. Accordingly, some common approach will need to be agreed.

6.6 *Taking another approach*

It is perfectly respectable to argue that this issue is all too difficult and that tackling it is likely to cause more problems than it solves.

That argument suggests that there is an inbuilt self-correcting mechanism. A combination of improving relative economic wage rates elsewhere in Europe and the wider world, an ever-increasing cost of housing and general living expenses in this country together with some environmental degradation – noise pollution, a reduction in open spaces etc – will lead people no longer to see this country as an attractive destination. As a result, the increase in population will first slow and then stop.

The drawback to this approach for those of us who make up the current settled population is that we may have to live for some time in 'stressed' social conditions to bring this rebalancing about.

6.7 *A vigorous public debate*

Wherever one stands in relation to the issue of population growth it is surely right that the risk-reward ratios of these various issues need to be explored and debated. The people of this country are entitled to have laid out before them the range of challenges and opportunities that demographic change will cause.

Given the apparent scale of that demographic change and the long-term impact of any policy decisions such a debate should begin sooner rather than later.

If this short pamphlet helps to initiate such a debate it will have served its purpose.

Bibliography

There is a huge range of information sources covering every aspect of this topic. The following is a short list of those most frequently used as background to this pamphlet.

Danny Dorling, *All that is Solid: The Great Housing Disaster*, 2014.

Laurence Smith, *The New North, the World in 2050*, 2011.

David Goodhart, *The British Dream, Success and Failures of Post-war Immigration*, 2014.

Stephen Emmott, *10 Billion*, 2013.

Paul Collier, *Exodus: How Migration is Changing our World*, 2013.

House of Lords Select Committee on Economic Affairs, *The Economic Impact of Immigration, 1st Report of Session 2007-2008*, April 2008.

Secretary of State for the Home Department, *Government reply to the report on the Economic Impact of Immigration by the House of Lords Committee on Economic Affairs*, June 2008.

House of Lords European Union Committee, *EU Action Plan against migrant smuggling*, November 2015.

House of Lords Select Committee on Public Service and Demographic Change, *Ready for Ageing?*, March 2013.

The Royal Society, *People and the Planet*, April 2012.

Migration Advisory Committee, *The growth if EU and non-EU labour in low-skilled jobs and its impact on the UK*, July 2014.

ONS, *2011 Census*, 2012.

Migration Advisory Committee, *Annual Report 2013/14*, November 2014.

Migration Watch, *An Assessment of the Fiscal Effects of Immigration to the UK*, March 2014.

Higher Education Commission, *Postgraduate Education*, November 2012.

Home Office, *Student Visitors, Research Report 71*, June 2013.

UN, World Population Prospects the 2012 Revision, June 2013.

ONS, *Childbearing among UK Born and Non-UK Born Women living in the UK*, October 2012.

Ipsos *MORI, Perception and Reality, 10 things we should know about attitudes to immigration in the UK*, January 2014.

Lord Goldsmith *QC, Citizenship Review*, 2008.

Countryside Survey, *Final Report for LCM 2007 the new UK Land Cover Map*, July 2011.

ONS, *Fifty Years of United Kingdom national population projections: how accurate have they been?*, 2007

Institution of Mechanical Engineers, *Population: One Planet. Too many People*, 2011.

Adair Turner, *Do We Need More Immigrants and Babies – Speech at LSE*. Published, 2007.

Appendix I: Expanded tables

Table AI.1: Sources of population increase in the year ending 30 June 2016[1]

		2016	Per day
Natural Increase (Excess of births over deaths)		193,000	529
Increase in armed forces		9,500	26
Immigration Flows inwards (arriving in UK)			
(A) From EU			
	EU 15	138,000	378
	EU 8	73,000	200
	EU 2	70,000	192
	Other	3,000	8
	Subtotal EU Arrivals	284,000	778
(B) From Elsewhere			
	Asia	178,000	488
	Africa	36,000	99
	Americas	35,000	96
	Oceania	22,000	60
	Total Elsewhere*	289,000	792
	Returning British	77,000	211
	Subtotal Non-EU arrivals	366,000	1,003
	Gross Immigration	650,000	1,781
Emigration Flows Outwards (leaving UK)			
	Emigrants – EU	(95,000)	(260)
	Emigrants – Non-EU	(93,000)	(255)
	Emigrants – British	(127,000)	(348)
	Total emigrants	(315,000)	(863)
	Net migration	335,000	920
Population Increase		538,500	1,475

*Supplementary to immigration from elsewhere, there was immigration of 17,000 from other European states and 1,000 immigrants who were regarded as stateless.
The ONS recently changed its method for categorising non-EU immigration/ emigration. It has replaced three categories (Old Commonwealth, New Commonwealth and Other) with a series of regionally based categories. So, with the above general figures, the key regions and their numbers also are detailed.

Table AI.2: Comparison with other major EU countries[2]

2013	2013 Population	Population Increase	Percentage Change	Population Density
EU (28 Countries)	505,166,839	1,106,494	0.22%	116.4 (Est.)
United Kingdom	63,905,297	409,994	0.65%	264.4
France	65,600,350	323,867	0.50%	103.9
Italy	59,685,227	291,020	0.49%	199.4
Germany	80,523,746	195,846	0.24%	225.8
Netherlands	16,779,575	49,227	0.29%	498.4

Table AI.3: Comparison with other major EU countries[2]

2014	2014 Population	Population Increase	Percentage Change	Population Density
EU (28 Countries)	506,973,868 (Est.)	1,807,029	0.36%	116.6 (Est.)
United Kingdom	64,351,155	445,858	0.70%	266.4
France	65,942,093	341,743	0.52%	104.5
Italy	60,782,668	1,097,441	1.8%	201.2
Germany	80,767,463	243,717	0.30%	226.6
Netherlands	16,829,289	49,714	0.29%	500.7

Table AI.4: Comparison with other major EU countries[2]

2015	2015 Population	Population Increase	Percentage Change	Population Density
EU (28 countries)	508,404,320 (Est.)	1,506,781	0.30%	117.1 (Est.)
United Kingdom	64,875,165 (Est.)	524,010	0.81%	268.6
France	66,488,186	546,093	0.83%	105.3
Italy	60,795,612	12,944	0.02%	201.0
Germany	81,197,537	430,074	0.53%	228.6
Netherlands	16,900,726	71,440	0.42%	502.9

Table AI.5: Comparison with other major EU countries[2]

2016	2016 Population	Population Increase	Percentage Change	Population Density (people per sq.km)
EU (28 countries)	510,284,430 (Est.)	1,880,110	0.37%	Not yet released by Eurostat
United Kingdom	65,382,556 (Est.)	507,391	0.78%	–
France	66,759,950	271,764	0.41%	–
Italy	60,665,551	–130,061	0.21%	–
Germany	82,175,684	978,147	1.2%	–
Netherlands	16,979,120	78,394	0.46%	–

Table AI.6: Constituent parts of population growth 1995-2015[3]

	1995	2000	2005	2010	2015
Natural Increase	90,170	68,450	139,585	245,605	171,800
Immigration					
EU 14/15	61,000	63,000	72,000	76,000	130,000
EU 8	N/A	N/A	77,000	86,000	73,000
EU 2	N/A	N/A	N/A	10,000	65,000
Other	0	0	3,000	4,000	2,000
Total EU	61,000	63,000	152,000	176,000	269,000
Commonwealth	85,000	147,000	180,000	187,000	116,000
Non-EU Non-Commonwealth	82,000	169,000	137,000	135,000	163,000
British	84,000	99,000	98,000	93,000	84,000
Total Non-EU	251,000	415,000	415,000	415,000	363,000
Total Immigration	312,000	479,000	567,000	591,000	631,000
Emigration					
EU 14/15	(38,000)	(57,000)	(40,000)	(58,000)	(50,000)
EU 8	N/A	N/A	(15,000)	(37,000)	(27,000)
EU2	N/A	N/A	N/A	(2,000)	(7,000)
Other	0	0	(1,000)	(1,000)	(1,000)
Total EU	(38,000)	(57,000)	(56,000)	(99,000)	(86,000)
Commonwealth	(29,000)	(48,000)	(60,000)	(52,000)	(42,000)
Non-EU Non-Commonwealth	(34,000)	(55,000)	(59,000)	(52,000)	(48,000)
British	(135,000)	(161,000)	(186,000)	(136,000)	(124,000)
Total Non-EU	(198,000)	(263,000)	(305,000)	(240,000)	(214,000)
Total Emigration	(236,000)	(321,000)	(361,000)	(339,000)	(299,000)
Net Immigration	76,000	158,000	267,000*	256,000*	332,000
Increase in Population	166,170	226,450	406,585	501,605	503,800

*Although the net migration figure does not fit the number created by taking away emigration from immigration these are the figures provided by the ONS.

Table AI.7: Comparison of French, German and British long term population projections (millions)[4]

	2015	2020	2030	2040	2050	2060	2070	2080	% Increase by 2080
France	66.4	67.8	70.5	72.9	74.4	75.5	76.9	78.7	18.5%
Germany	81.2	83.8	84.6	84.1	82.7	80.8	79.2	77.8	(−4.2%)
United Kingdom	64.9	67.2	71.6	75.5	75.0	79.3	81.0	82.4	27.0%

Table AI.8: Comparison of French, German and British long term population density projections (persons per sq.km)[5]

	2015	2020	2030	2040	2050	2060	2070	2080	% Increase by 2080
France	105.3	107.2	111.4	115.2	117.5	119.3	121.6	121.2	15.1%
Germany	228.6	234.4	236.8	235.4	231.4	226.2	221.9	217.7	(−4.8%)
United Kingdom	268.6	270.5	288.1	301.8	312.1	319.2	325.8	331.7	23.5%

Appendix II: Author's calculations

1. **Author's calculation of the UK's population density in 2039.**
   Dividing the principal ONS projection for the UK's population in 2039 (74.3m)[1] over the UK's area size (243,269 sq.km)[2] = 74,300,000/243,269 = 305 persons per sq. km

2. **Author's calculation of the UK's population density in 2039 if their 'high' projection is more accurate.**
   Dividing the 'high' ONS projection for the UK's population in 2039 (79.1m)[3] over the UK's area size (243,269)[4] = 79,100,000/243,269 = 325 persons per sq. km

3. **Author's calculation of England's population density in 2039.**
   Dividing the principal ONS projection for the England's population in 2039 (63.3m)[5] over England's area size (130,308)[6] = 63,282,000/130,308 = 486 persons per sq. km

4. **Author's calculation of England's population density in 2039 if the ONS 'high' projection is more accurate.**
   Dividing the 'high' ONS projection for the England's population in 2039 (67.2m)[7] over England's area size (130,308)[8] = 67,159,000/130,308 = 515 persons per sq. km.

5. **Authors calculation of England's projected population density in 2050.**
   Proportion of England's population of the United Kingdom (June 2015) = 54,786,327 out of 65,110,034 = 84.14%.[9] Using the Eurostat forecast of UK population at 75.0m by 2050, and the current proportion of England's population of the United Kingdom, one can roughly estimate England's population. 75,000,000/100 = 750,0000. 750,000*84.14 = 63,108,000 persons. That can then be then divided by England's current size in sq. km to create a

population density forecast. 63,108,000 people/ 130,308 sq. km[10] = 484 persons per sq. km.

6. **Authors calculation of England's projected population density in 2080.**

   Using the previous calculation of the proportion of England's population of the United Kingdom, the figure for 2080 can be calculated. The Eurostat forecasted population for the United Kingdom for 2080 is 82.4m. The calculation for England's proportion follows, 82,400,000/100 = 824,0000. 824,000*84.14 = 69,330,000 persons. That can then be then divided by England's current size in sq. km to create a population density forecast. 69,330,000 people/ 130,308 sq. km[11] = 532 persons per sq. km

7. **Authors calculations of French, German and British long term population density projections (persons per sq.km).**

   Eurostat provides a population projection for France, Germany and Britain for each decade until 2080.[12] These projections have then been divided by the current area size of each country, these have also been provided by Eurostat.[13]

Notes

Introduction

1 ONS, *Population estimates for UK, England, Wales, Scotland and Northern Ireland: mid-2016*, June 2017.
2 ONS, *2011 Census: Population and household estimates for the United Kingdom, March 2011*, March 2013.
3 ONS, *Childbearing of UK and non-UK born women living in the UK, 2011 Census data*, February 2014.
4 ONS, *National Population Projections: 2014-based*, October 2015.

1. Clarifying the Terms of Debate

1 Voltaire, *The Philosophical Works*, 2016, (eBook: e-artnow).
2 The Migration Observatory, *Migrants in the UK: An Overview*, February 2017
3 UNESCO, *United Nations Convention Migrants' Rights*, 2005.
4 ONS, *Population estimates for UK, England, Wales, Scotland and Northern Ireland: mid-2016*, June 2017. ONS, Provisional Long-Term International Migration estimates, May 2017.
5 House of Commons Committee of Public Account, *e-Borders and successor programmes Twenty-seventh Report of Session 2015-2016*. Published: February 2016.
6 Home Office, *Immigration statistics, October to December 2013*, February 2014.
7 Home Office, *Migrant journey: fifth report*, February 2015.
8 ONS, *Migration Statistics Quarterly Report: August 2016*, August 2016.
9 Eurostat, *Fertility Statistics, Table 1: TFR, 1960-2015*, March 2017.
10 A. Berrington, L. Waller and J. Rayner, *New Insights into the fertility patterns of recent Polish migrants in the United Kingdom*, Journal of Population Research, Vol 31, Issue 2, June 2014.
11 L. Waller (openpop.org), *Is the Fertility of Polish Women Higher in the UK than in Poland?* Published: March 2014.
12 ONS, *Births in England and Wales by Parents' Country of Birth: 2011*, August 2012.
13 ONS, *How many babies born in England and Wales have mothers from other European Union countries?* Published: February 2014.
14 The Migration Observatory, *Briefing: Impact of Population Growth*, February 2016.
15 The Migration Observatory, *Report: Migration and Population Growth*, September 2012.

16 ONS, *Population estimates for UK, England, Wales, Scotland and Northern Ireland: mid-2016*, June 2017.

17 ONS, *National Population Projections: 2014-based*, October 2015.

18 ONS, *Population estimates for UK, England, Wales, Scotland and Northern Ireland: mid-2016*, June 2017.

19 ONS, *Population Density Tables*. Published June 2015. ONS, *Population estimates for UK, England, Wales, Scotland and Northern Ireland: mid-2016*, June 2017.

20 ONS, *Annual Mid year population estimates: 2013*, June 2014.

2. How did we get to where we are?

1 ONS, Fertility, *2014-based national population projections reference volume*, March 2016.

2 ONS, *Net migration to the UK has increased, according to latest estimates (Figure 1 in bulletin)*, February 2014.

3 ONS, *Changes in UK population over the last 50 years*, June 2014.

4 Populationpyramind.net, *United Kingdom*, 2017.

5 ONS, *Dataset: Long-term international migration 2.01a, citizenship, UK and England and Wales*, December 2016.

6 ONS, *The Changing UK Population*, January 2015.

7 ONS, Fertility, *2014-based national population projections reference volume*, March 2016.

3. Future levels of UK population

1 ONS, *2011 Census: Population Estimates for the United Kingdom, March 2011*, December 2012.

2 ONS, *Dataset: Table A1-1, Principal Projection – UK Summary*, October 2015. ONS, *Dataset: Z1 – Zipped Population Projections Data Files, UK*, October 2015.

3 National Statistics and Government Actuary's Department, *National Population Projections 2000 based*, 2002.

4 ONS, *National Life Tables, United Kingdom: 2012-2014*, September 2015.

5 ONS, *National Population Projections: 2014-based Statistical Bulletin*, October 2015.

6 ONS, *Dataset: Table A1-1, Principal Projection – UK Summary*, October 2015.

7 ONS, *National Population Projections: 2014-based Statistical Bulletin*, October 2015.

8 A. Kirk, 'Aging Britain: One in 12 will be aged over 80 by 2039', *The Daily Telegraph*, October 2015.

9 ONS, *Population estimates for UK, England, Wales, Scotland and Northern Ireland: mid-2016*, June 2017.

10 Author's calculation of the UK's population density in 2039 – see Appendix II, point 1.

11 Author's calculation of the UK's population density in 2039 if the ONS 'high' projection is more accurate – Appendix II, point 2.

12 Author's calculation of England's population density in 2039 – see Appendix II, point 3.

13 Author's calculation of England's population density in 2039 if the ONS 'high' projection is more accurate – Appendix II, point 4.

14 Authors calculation of England's projected population in 2080 – see Appendix II, point 5.

15 Author's calculation of England's projected population in 2050 – see Appendix II, point 6.

4. Implications for our communities

1 ONS, *Population estimates for UK, England, Wales, Scotland and Northern Ireland: mid-2016,* June 2017.

2 A. Bound and C. Tighe, 'Northern Powerhouse project threatened by "brain drain"', *Financial* Times, April 2016.

3 ONS, *Subnational Population Projections for Local Authorities in England: Table 2,* May 2016.

4 NRS, *Population Projections for Scottish Areas (2014-based,* October 2016.

5 Department for Communities and Local Government, *Live tables on household projections,* July 2016.

6 National Records of Scotland, *Household projections for Scotland, 2014 based,* January 2017.

7 TAYplan, *Proposed Strategic Development Plan,* May 2015.

8 Opinion Research Services and Various Councils, *Strategic Housing Assessment (SHMA) for Central Norfolk,* January 2016.

9 Opinion Research Services and Stockton-On-Tees Borough Council, *Stockton-On-Tees Strategic Housing Market Assessment 2016,* November 2016.

10 GL Hearn and Guildford Borough Council, *West Surrey Strategic Housing Market Assessment: Guildford Addendum Report 2017,* March 2017.

5. Why increase our population?

1 European Commission, *European Economic Forecast – Autumn 2015,* November 2015.

2 House of Lords Select Committee on Economic Affairs, *The Economic Impact of Immigration, 1st Report of Session 2007-2008,* April 2008.

3 A. Presse (NDTV Sports), *FA may limit foreign players in English Premier League,* May 2014. L. Taylor and M. Adamson, 'Revealed: The Premier League reaches an all-time low of English players', *The Guardian,* August 2013.

4 Migration Advisory Committee, *News Release: Migration Advisory Committee recommends limited retention of nurses on shortage occupation list,* March 2016.

5 C. Giles, What has the EU done for the UK?, *Financial Times,* March 2017.

6 C. Rienzo (National Institute of Economic and Social Research), *What's the link between labour productivity and immigration in the UK?,* November 2013.

7 C. Giles, 'UK workers' productivity stuck below pre-crisis level', *Financial Times,* April 2017.

8 The Migration Observatory, *The labour market effects of immigration,* February 2017.

9   G. Rzevski, 'Letters to the Editor: Low productivity', *The Times*, June 2017.
10 UN Department of Economic and Social Affairs, Population Division, *World Population Prospects: The 2017 Revision, custom data acquired via website*, 2017.
11 D. Attenborough (Church and State), *David Attenborough's speech to the RSA: People and Planet*, March 2011.
12 A. Turner (LSE), *The Ageing Society: challenges opportunities and unnecessary scares*, April 2007.
13 C. Barrett, 'London property market problems can't be blamed on Brexit vote', *Financial Times*, April 2016.
14 A. Ellson and G. Swerling, 'Nearly 300 flats and just two occupied by British owners', *The Times*, April 2017.
15 Lloyds Bank, *Lloyds Bank Affordable Cities Review*, March 2015.
16 HM Treasury, *Budget 2016*, March 2016.
17 JLT Employee Benefits, *For every £1 contributed in a DB pension, deficits have grown by £2.34*, March 2016.
18 HM Treasury, *Budget 2016*, March 2016.
19 S. Nickell and J. Saleheen (Bank of England), *The impact of immigration on occupational wages: evidence from Britain*, December 2015

6. Concluding thoughts

1   D. H. Meadows, D. L. Meadows, J. Rangers and W. W. Behrens III, *The limits to growth – a report for the Club of Rome's project on the predicament of mankind*, 1972.
2   T. Macalister, 'Oil: future world shortages are being drastically underplayed, say experts', *The Guardian*, November 2009.
3   The World Bank, *Age Dependency Ratio*, 2017.
4   *Ibid.*
5   L. Lewis, 'Age survey underlines pressures on Japan', *Financial Times*, May 2016.
6   N. Watt and P. Wintour, 'How immigration came to haunt Labour: the inside story', *The Guardian*, March 2015.
7   Comptroller and Auditor General of National Audit Office, *E-borders and successor programmes*, December 2015.
8   gov.scot, *Purpose Targets*, June 2017.

Appendix I: Expanded tables

1   ONS, *Population estimates for UK, England, Wales, Scotland and Northern Ireland: mid-2016*, June 2017. ONS, Provisional Long-Term International Migration estimates, May 2017.
2   Eurostat, *Table: Population Density*, June 2017. Eurostat, *Population on 1 January*, June 2017.
3   ONS, *Dataset: Long-term international migration 2.01a, citizenship, UK and England and Wales*, December 2016. ONS, *Overview of the UK Population: March 2017*, March 2017.

4   Eurostat, *Table: Population projections*, June 2017.
5   *Ibid.* Authors calculation of French, German and British long term population density projections (persons per sq.km) – see appendix 2 No. 7.

Appendix II: Author's calculations

1   ONS, *National Population Projections: 2014-based Statistical Bulletin*, October 2015

2   ONS, *Population estimates for UK, England, Wales, Scotland and Northern Ireland: mid-2016*, June 2017.

3   ONS, *National Population Projections: 2014-based Statistical Bulletin*, October 2015

4   ONS, *Population estimates for UK, England, Wales, Scotland and Northern Ireland: mid-2016*, June 2017.

5   ONS, *Dataset: Table A1-4, Principal Projection – England Summary*, October 2015.

6   ONS, *Population estimates for UK, England, Wales, Scotland and Northern Ireland: mid-2016*, June 2017.

7   ONS, *Dataset: Table H1-4, High Population Projection – England Summary*, October 2015.

8   ONS, *Population estimates for UK, England, Wales, Scotland and Northern Ireland: mid-2016*, June 2017.

9   ONS, *Population estimates for UK, England, Wales, Scotland and Northern Ireland: mid-2016*, June 2017.

10 *Ibid.*

11 *Ibid.*

12 Eurostat, *Table: Population projections*, June 2017.

13 Eurostat, *Table: Area by NUTS 3 Region*, May 2017.